Knots

Knots

THE KNOTS YOU NEED AND HOW TO TIE THEM

RYDON
PUBLISHING

A Rydon Publishing Book
35 The Quadrant
Hassocks
West Sussex
BN6 8BP

www.rydonpublishing.co.uk
www.rydonpublishing.com

First published by Rydon Publishing in 2019

A CIP catalogue record for this book is available from the British Library.

ISBN: 978-1-910821-28-2

Printed in Poland by BZGraf S.A.

CONTENTS

"Whatever your relationship with knots, whether you use them for work or just for adventure sports, this book is a great aid to keep you safe and heighten your knowledge."

People often ask me what I would take in a survival situation. As a short and simple answer, I often say that I would take a knife. However, the longer more detailed answer would be that the greatest tools you can have in a survival situation are both knowledge and experience. Knowledge of what to do and what to prioritize and experience of doing it in the context that it is needed.

For example, tying a Clove Hitch in your sitting room is vastly different from tying one on the side of a mountain in minus ten degrees when it's blowing a hooley! So I recommend that you use this book to form the foundation of your knowledge whilst remembering that it's important to practice in the right context.

When working in the adventure industry, whether tying knots for safety, personal climbing or taking clients on survival missions and tying that last lashing of a makeshift shelter, the common theme is that knots don't lie. If it doesn't look right that's because it is not right. There are no grey areas when it comes to tying a knot.

Learning the contents of this book will help you to become confident so that when your time comes to put them to the test, whether that's sailing, climbing or in a real life survival situation, you will have the knowledge and composure to execute that knot!

*Tim Treloar is the owner of **TTAdventures** – an outdoor company that specializes in training, education and consultancy to a range of clients across the globe. He is a qualified leader in a range of adventure pursuits including caving, climbing and mountaineering.*

Tim has worked in TV both as a presenter and outdoor safety consultant for ITV, CITV and Channel 4. Tim worked as an on-screen instructor on series 1 and 2 of the BAFTA-winning Survival School with Bear Grylls.

Tim has also completed a range of extreme adventure challenges for the likes of Macmillan and Help for Heroes. One challenge saw him running, self-supported, six marathons in five days across the Atacama desert in Chile.

Great thanks are due to the editorial team at Rydon Publishing and to Tim Treloar from **TTAdventures** for creating this book. Special thanks to Olivia Huse who spent hours researching, drafting and tying every knot, designer Pru Rogers and editor Verity Graves-Morris.

We hope that this book is a timeless resource for all of your adventurous pursuits – whether it's nautical knots, sailing adventures or hitches for camping or climbing expeditions.

Robert Ertle
Rydon Publishing Limited

FOR YOUR SAFETY

INTRODUCTION

Knots are an essential part of our everyday life, just as they were to our ancestors and their ancestors before them. They have played a crucial role in human development throughout the years with their clear advantages not only in hunting and survival, but also in rescue, transport, fishing, climbing and decoration. This handbook contains clear illustrations and thorough step-by-step instructions that will allow any reader to practice over 50 different knots. The knots range in purpose and intensity and cover anything from Alpine Butterfly to Zeppelin Bend, with everything in between.

So, if you want to make a rope ladder with your children, sail the seas, safely climb mountains or make a True Lovers' Knot then this book has every knot you should need to know.

Knots is categorized into eight distinct sections –
Useful Knots, Stopper Knots, Fixed Loop Knots,
Crossing Knots, Hitches, Bends and Bowlines, Decorative
and Other Important Knots. All serve a different purpose,
but the helpful key will tell you exactly which activity each
knot is most suited to.

Climbing/
Mountaineering

Sailing

Camping/
Survival

Fishing

Decorative

Pioneering

These knots are intended for a multitude of uses
and the easy-to-follow instructions make this book
perfect for everyone, no matter what their ability.

Whether you are an expert or a novice, the aim of the book is to perfect your knot tying ability to suit your needs. The tying of a knot may be very straightforward (such as with an Overhand Knot) or it can be quite complicated (such as a Monkey's Fist). Therefore, each knot is accompanied by a number to represent their complexity.

(1) = Beginner

(2) = Intermediate

(3) = Difficult

It is also important to note that tying knots accurately requires an understanding of the type of material being used, for example cord, string, nylon webbing etc, as this will affect the knot. If you are using cotton string, for example, it may be very small and easy to tie, while stiff rope will be very difficult to tie, and may come apart once secured.

UNDERSTANDING THE BASICS OF ROPE WORK

Standing end   The end of the rope that is not active in knot tying.

Working end (w)   The end of the rope actively used in knot tying.

Loop   A complete turn of rope with a cross-over.

Bight   An incomplete loop that does not cross-over itself.

Turn   The U-shape that is formed when a rope is hung over a rail.

Round turn   A complete turn of rope around another object.

Frap   A wrapping turn made between two spars to tighten a lashing.

Hitch   A type of knot used to tie a rope to an object.

Bend   A type of knot used to join two ropes together.

Whipping   The securing of rope ends to prevent unravelling or fraying.

Splicing   The interweaving of rope ends to permanently join two ropes.

Start simple, begin by tying some of the easier knots before going on to the more elaborate ones.

Practice, practice, practice! Just as sailors did during long journeys, your knot tying skills will improve with time and repetition.

Before cutting any length of rope, first wrap tape or thin rope around the section you intend to cut. This will prevent it from fraying.

Always leave yourself enough length to have a long tail, as this will help work the knot tight.

Bowline

KNOT

The **Bowline Knot** is quick and simple to tie, and
it forms the basis of many more complicated variations
such as the Portuguese Bowline and Bowline on a Bight.
It creates a fixed loop at the end of a rope which can
withstand a heavy load without slipping or jamming.
Without a load, this knot is easy to untie, making it a
preferential knot for sailors and adventurers.
The Bowline is often referred to by knot enthusiasts as
the King of the Knots because of its versatility.

1.

Loop the rope until it is almost double the length of your desired final loop.

2.

Thread the working end through the back of the loop.

3.

Pass the working end behind the standing part.

4.

Bring the working end through the front of the loop and pull the knot tight.

5.

The finished Bowline will hold tight unless loosened by forcing up the bight holding the standing end.

2

Bowline
ON A BIGHT

Just as the name suggests, the **Bowline on a Bight** is an adaptation of the Bowline for use in the middle of a rope. If tied correctly, the knot will secure two fixed and dependable loops and is often commended for its strengths as a knot in climbing and rescue situations. As far as useful knots go, this is a knot you simply must know. It is quick to tie, can be untied easily even after significant strain, and does not rely on having access to a rope end, unlike most other knots.

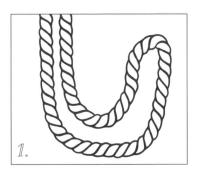

1.

Create a U-shaped bight in the middle of the accessible rope so that the rope is doubled back on itself.

2.

Make an overhand loop to pass the end of the bight up through. Ensure that the loop created is the final size that you require.

3.

Open the end of doubled rope and take it around the entire knot.

4.

Pass the rope around the knot and pull flat. Tighten to secure the knot.

1

Clove
HITCH

The **Clove Hitch,** or Double Hitch, is an effective all-purpose knot that is used to attach a rope to a post or carabiner. It was first named by *Falconer's Universal Dictionary of the Marine* in 1769, but paintings date it back as far as the early sixteenth century for its use on ratlines. Today it is most commonly used as the foundation for lashing.
It is a good binding knot but can be susceptible to slipping if constant pressure is not maintained on the rope.

1.

Turn the working end once around the object.

2.

Cross the working end over the standing part and pass around the object to create one half turn.

3.

Thread the working end back towards the cross-over and through the loop between the rope and the object.

4.

Work the hitch tight, ensuring that the standing part and working end are against each other.

1

Figure of Eight
KNOT

The **Figure of Eight** is a knot that most are familiar with, even if there are uncertainties about how to tie it. Otherwise referred to as the Flemish Bend, the knot first came into recorded use with its application in running rigging over 200 years ago. It is a stopper knot that has many practical applications, making it popular in climbing, sailing and fishing.

With an additional piece of rope, the knot can be easily adapted into a Figure of Eight Bend by threading the second rope through, parallel to the existing line. If the knot is kept flat, it should create a neat bend.

Form a bight in the standing end of rope and pass it over itself to create a loop.

Tuck the working end beneath the standing part to form a figure of eight shape.

Thread the end through the top loop, pulling it all the way through.

Optional: Leave a loop in the knot if you require a quick release.

Pull the two ends in opposite directions to tighten and to complete it.

1

Overhand KNOT

The **Overhand Knot,** or Thumb Knot is the most basic of all knots and is essential to know as it often forms the basis of more advanced knots. Being a stopper knot, the Overhand prevents the fraying and unravelling of a rope when tied in an end, making it valuable in all trades.

It can be tied directly against another knot or object and holds fast, making it great for occasions when a permanent knot is needed. However, it is difficult to untie and can jam badly.

1.

Make a basic loop in the rope.

2.

Pass the working end up through the bight and through the formed loop.

3.

Work the knot tight by pulling on each end.

1

Reef
KNOT

The **Reef Knot** is one of the oldest binding knots which was
traditionally used by sailors to 'reef' their sails while at sea.
It is unique in that it can be tied and tightened at both ends,
making it versatile for securing a rope around an object.
It is commonly used for tying shoelaces and is often
taught with the chant:
"Left over right and tuck under,
Right over left and tuck under"
This knot is most reliable when using two ropes of the
same thickness but can untie very easily if either end is
jerked out to the side.

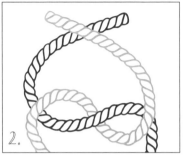

Using two ropes, hold the working end of each rope in each hand. Pass the working end of the left rope over the right rope, and tuck under.

Take the working end of the right rope, lay it over the rope in your left hand, and tuck under.

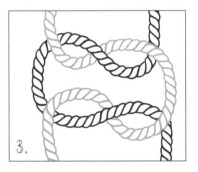

Pull all of the ends tight to fasten.

If only one end is pulled, the knot can capsize and become undone.

Rolling HITCH

The best general-purpose hitch would have to be the **Rolling Hitch** for its ability to be tied and untied whilst withstanding strain on the rope. It does not bind and, when tied correctly, does not slip. The Rolling Hitch is often used to tie a rope to a larger rope or object such as a pole or rod, to grip it.

The knot is most reliable for use in natural fibre as opposed to synthetic ropes. It is important that this hitch must always be put on a rope against the lay as it only grips in one direction.

1.

Pass the end of the thinner rope around the thicker rope or object.

2.

Take the working end around the rope or object and over itself diagonally from right to left.

3.

Repeat to form another diagonal turn to the right of the one made in Step 2.

4.

Take the working end around the object once more, before tucking under itself.

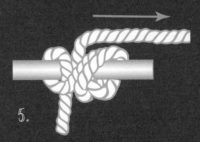

5.

The rope will grip securely when pulled in one direction but will slip when pulled in the other.

2

Round Turn
& TWO HALF HITCHES

A **Round Turn and Two Half Hitches** gets its name from the build-up of the knot, making it easy to remember! The Round Turn completely encircles the object and the Two Half Hitches have the effect of locking the knot, meaning that it is a secure knot if tied and tightened correctly. This knot is used for attaching a rope to an object such as a ring or post making it popular amongst sailors, climbers and campers. Advantages of the Round Turn and Two Half Hitches is that it is easy to tie and untie, and it is self-tightening.

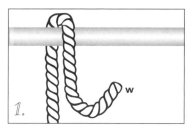

Wrap the working end around an object.

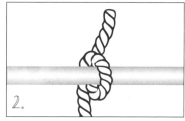

Make another complete turn of the rope around the object.

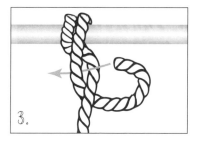

Thread the rope over the standing end, around it and back through to form a half hitch.

Repeat Step 3 to form a second half hitch. If wishing to use up surplus line or to increase security, make additional half hitches around the standing end.

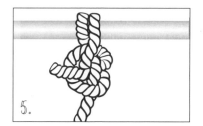

Push the knot towards the object to tighten and complete the knot.

Sheet
BEND

As far as bends go, the **Sheet Bend** is the most reliable in joining two ropes of different diameters without any risk of them slipping when tied correctly. It is an easy knot to tie, making it popular amongst sailors and fishermen, and can be secured further by ensuring that both working ends are on the same side of the finished knot. When the ropes are significantly different in thickness, it is recommended to reinforce the knot by adding another round turn and forming a Double Sheet Bend.

1.

Make a bight in the thicker rope and hold it closed.

2.

Pass the working end of the thinner rope behind the thicker rope and through the bight.

3.

Bring the working end of the thinner line around the neck of the bight.

4.

Pass the thinner rope beneath its own standing part and pull tight. For maximum security, check that both ends are on the same side.

2

Double Sheet
BEND

The **Double Sheet Bend** follows on from the Sheet Bend and is preferential if two ropes have a marked difference in their diameters or rigidity, or synthetic ropes are being used.
This bend is most commonly used by sailors and fishermen and, like the Sheet Bend, is used to join two ropes of different thicknesses. It is also used in tying the jib sheets with the clew of the sail.

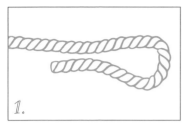

Make a bight in the thicker rope and hold it closed.

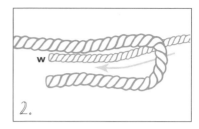

Pass the working end of the thinner rope behind the thicker rope and through the bight.

Bring the working end of the thinner line around the neck of the bight.

Pass the thinner rope beneath its own standing part and pull tight so that both ends are on the same side.

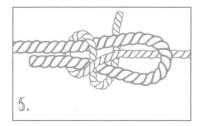

Take a second turn around the bight which will reinforce the knot.

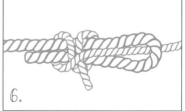

Tuck the working end beneath its own standing part. Work the loops tight against the bight to secure.

Heaving Line
KNOT

The **Heaving Line Knot** is part of a family of knots used for adding weight to the end of a line which makes lines easier to direct when being thrown. Originally it was used by sailors to throw lines from one boat to another, whereas today it has generally taken on a more decorative purpose. The number of wraps required is optional and will depend on the length of your line.

1.

Make two bights alongside each other in opposite directions. The bights should be similar in size, with the working end long enough to tie the knot.

2.

Thread the working end through the bight from beneath and wrap it around the bottom two strands.

3.

Now wrap the working end tightly, clockwise around all three strands of the rope.

4.

Continue wrapping the working end until it covers the length of the bights.

5.

Pass the working end through the exposed loop at the bottom bight.

6.

Pull the standing end of the rope to tighten and secure the rope into a neat Heaving Line knot.

3

Monkey's Fist
KNOT

The **Monkey's Fist** is a variation on the Heaving Line knot, originally designed to add weight to the end of a line to allow for more accurate throwing. Traditionally, it would have been tied around a stone or pebble to add greater weight, but as its purpose has become more decorative this is not so common.

The name derives from the appearance of the knot, with the finished knot resembling a small, clenched fist. It is the most common knot to be used in a pair of cufflinks or earrings and is often used in home furnishing, particularly as curtain pulls or to add a decorative finish.

Wrap three turns of the same size in a length of rope. Hold them together to form a three-line coil.

Make an extra three turns at a 90° angle, wrapping around the existing coil. If you wish to insert a weight, you should do it now.

Thread the working end around one side of the first coil. Make three turns around the second coil by passing the rope inside the first coil.

Take the working end up through the second coil on one side, and then thread it down past the second coil on the opposite side. Wrap one final turn up through the two coils whilst maintaining the knot's structure.

Thread the working end through and out of the knot so that it stands on the opposite side to the standing part.

Pull each part of the cord by starting at one end and working the loose rope through the knot. Trim the working end to neaten.

2

Double Overhand
KNOT

The Overhand Knot can be modified simply by adding an extra pass to create the **Double Overhand**, or two further passes to create the Triple Overhand. The knots are all effective as stoppers to prevent a line pulling through a hole or anchor point, making them popular in climbing, sailing and fishing.

The Double Overhand has a more sinister history and is also known as the Blood Knot when tied in a Cat O'Nine Tails.

1.

Tie an overhand knot by forming a loop with the line.

2.

Pass the working end over the standing part and through the back of the loop created by the overhand knot.

3.

Slide the knot into position towards the end of the line. Be sure to leave some tail sticking out from the end of the knot.

4.

Pull to tighten.

1

Stevedore

KNOT

Traditionally used by stevedores, the **Stevedore Knot** is a reliable knot used as a stopper by dockworkers in the unloading and loading of cargo onto ships. The knot's ability to hoist heavy loads without slipping or jamming made it extremely popular right up until cranes were introduced.

The Stevedore is a useful knot to know as it is moderately bulky, making it more practical than other stopper knots. It is relatively simple to tie, initially following the same steps as a Figure of Eight knot before adding an extra wrap.

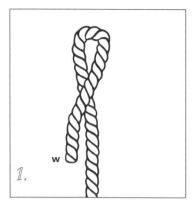

1.

Take the working end over the standing part of the rope.

2.

Turn the end twice until the line has crossed itself at four points.

3.

Thread the working end through the largest loop.

4.

Push the turn towards the loop before tightening.

The **Alpine Butterfly** is generally used when neither end of rope is available and provides a secure loop in the middle of a rope. It retains great strength when pulled in any different direction and is suitable for any type of rope or line, making it hugely versatile. It is often used to isolate a damaged piece of rope, and for this purpose is highly recommended over the Sheepshank.
The knot gets its name from the symmetricity and resemblance to a butterfly.

1.

Pass the line over your hand.

2.

Continue to wrap the end around your hand until you have three complete turns.

3.

Take the leftmost loop over the other two, moving towards the right.

4.

Repeat to bring the new leftmost loop over the other two.

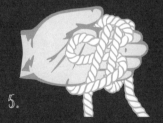

5.

Tuck this loop back beneath the other loops.

6.

Slide the rope off your hand and pull the middle loop out through the other two loops. Pull to tighten.

1

Figure of Eight
LOOP

The **Figure of Eight Loop**, not to be confused with the Figure of Eight Knot, is a knot created by a loop on a bight. It is best for enduring light to moderate rope strain but can become jammed or hard to untie under a heavy load. The diameter of the knot should be kept small for use in climbing or fishing to avoid being caught, as this can jeopardize the knot's integrity.

1.

Make a narrow bight in the line by folding the rope in half.

2.

Turn the bight into a loop by passing the working end over the standing end.

3.

Pass this working end under the standing end to make a second double loop of the figure of eight.

4.

Thread the eye of the bight through the first loop from front to back and pull through.

5.

Adjust the eye of the bight to size by tightening the knot. There should be no unnecessary twists in the rope for maximum security.

The **Overhand Loop** is the fastest and simplest way to form a fixed loop on a line. It is beneficially tied on a bight, meaning that access to the ends of a rope are not required. However, this knot can become very tight and after exposure to heavy strain it can become difficult to untie, so it might not be the best-suited fixed loop in all situations. Popular with campers, this knot can be multi-functional as a loop or a stopper knot.

1.

Make a narrow bight in the line by folding the rope in half.

2.

Take the end of the bight over the standing end and tuck it through the loop that has been created.

3.

Pull the loop through the hole and tighten.

Perfection

LOOP

Contrary to the name, the **Perfection Loop** is not perfect in all situations, but it is particularly useful in fly-fishing, hence its alternate name as the Angler's Loop. It is one of the easiest knots to create a small loop completely adjacent to the standing part of the rope or line. Successful tying of this knot will create a very secure loop in a rope, which can be either tied by itself or through a ring. If you want to secure this knot to a ring, pass the working end in Step 1 through the point of attachment after passing beneath the loop.

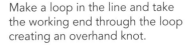

Make a loop in the line and take the working end through the loop creating an overhand knot.

Create a loop in the working end (if required thread through an attachment). Thread the working end up through the middle of the knot.

Pass the working end behind the standing line threading through the overhand loop and beneath its own part.

Tighten the knot and cut any excess working end to neaten.

2

Portuguese
BOWLINE

The **Portuguese Bowline** is renowned for its use in rescue situations, as the knot makes an excellent and adjustable body harness. In the case of an emergency, it can support a person seated in one loop, with the other loop providing support for the arms and chest. Additionally, this variation of the Bowline can be used to distribute strain when trying to move a heavy load, lessening the wear on a rope.

1.
Make a small loop.

2.
Pass the working end through the back of the small loop to form a larger loop.

3.
Use the working end to form a second large loop in front of the first and pass the working end through the back of the smaller loop.

4.
Thread the working end around the back of the standing part, and down through the smaller loop.

5.
Work the knot tight to get the large loops to a comparable size. The small loop should grip the working end.

1

Clove Hitch
ON A BIGHT

Tying a **Clove Hitch on a Bight** is often a much quicker method than using the working end. It can be made more secure by adding half hitches, in just the same manner as the second loop was added. As with the traditional Clove Hitch, this knot should be tied with caution as it can become loosened if continuous pressure is not maintained on the line.

The word "clove" originates from "cloven", meaning to split or divide.

1.

Form an overhand loop in the bight.

2.

Make another second loop in the same way as the first, in the same direction.

3.

Pass the right loop behind the left loop so that they overlap.

4.

Place the formed Clove Hitch over the post or rail and pull both ends to tighten the knot around the post.

Gripping
SAILOR'S HITCH

The **Gripping Sailor's Hitch** is often incorrectly named as the Sailor's Gripping Hitch, which causes confusion. The knot is effective in attaching one rope to another rope, pole or object to allow a lengthwise pull. Compared to similar hitches, the Gripping Sailor's Hitch has the greatest holding power.

This knot is one of the few knots in which old, thinner rope is recommended for tying as they have a rougher surface that increases friction. The gripper line should be smaller in diameter than the line being gripped.

1.

Make five complete turns of the line around the object side-by-side.

2.

Diagonally cross the turns and bring the working end around the object and in front of the standing part.

3.

Wrap the working end around the back of the object, completing a half turn before threading it through the first loop.

4.

Tighten by pulling on the standing part.

1

Ground-Line
HITCH

The **Ground-Line Hitch** is a secure knot often used to attach a rope to an anchor point. It works well with most types of rope, and its stability is not affected in wet conditions. Historically, it was used by fishermen to attach nets to the ground-line, a weighted rope on the bottom of the net, which is where the knot's name originates from. Today, the most common use of the Ground-Line Hitch is for securing fenders onto boats.

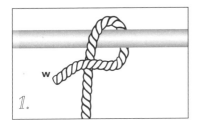

Pass the rope around the post or rail to complete a full turn.

Cross the line diagonally right to left over the object.

Create a half turn of the post.

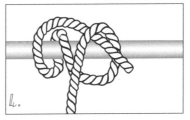

Tuck the working end through the first loop.

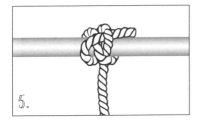

Pull the working end and standing end in opposite directions to secure the knot.

Snuggle

HITCH

The **Snuggle Hitch** is a modification of the Clove Hitch but is preferential for its increased strength and stability. By having stacked crossings, this knot has greater friction than the familiar Clove Hitch. Additionally, it is advantageous in that it can be tied at either end of the rope, or in the bight.

Originally devised by Owen Nuttall of West Yorkshire, it was only documented for the first time by the International Guild of Knot Tyers in *Knotting Matters*, published in 1987.

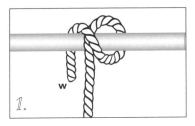

Wrap the line around a pole or object once, making a complete full turn.

Bring the working end over the front of the standing line.

Bring the working end up through the loop.

Turn the working end around the pole.

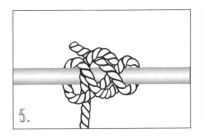

Bringing the working end diagonally from right to left up through the middle loop (standing part).

Pull to tighten the knot, ensuring that it is snug against the pole.

2

Square LASHING

Square Lashing is the easiest way to secure two poles at a right angle to each other. Lashings hold permanently and use multiple windings to fasten items together with cord. However, it is important that the windings aren't too tight, as too much tension on poles could cause them to bend or snap. When winding, successful lashings will pass on the inside of the previous turn if the turn occurs beneath a pole; and outside the previous turn if the rope passed over a pole on its last turn.

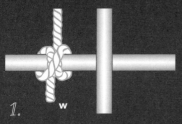

1.

Tie a Clove Hitch on the horizontal rod by the join to the vertical rod. Ensure that you have a long working end to tie this knot.

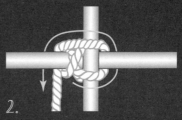

2.

Make a turn around both poles by running around the front of the lower vertical pole, behind the horizontal pole, around the front of the upper vertical pole and behind the existing knot.

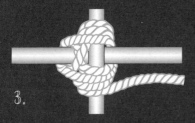

3.

Repeat the winding process three to four times, depending on the diameter of the poles and the thickness of the cord used.

4.

Frap to secure the existing windings by making a turn over the upper vertical pole and weaving clockwise between the poles. Repeat until you have two complete frapping turns.

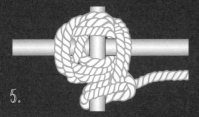

5.

Stopping on the horizontal pole, tie a secure Clove Hitch around the pole to prevent the lashing sliding under tension.

3

Boom
HITCH

The **Boom Hitch,** otherwise known as the Decorative Hitch, is one of the simplest knots to tie and it produces a neat knot which has many applications. The multiple turns in the knot ensure that it can withstand significant tension, and it is commonly regarded as a knot which is almost impossible to break. Adding more turns wil also increase the strength of this hitch. If this knot needs to be untied, finishing it with a bight tucked under makes for easier removal. Remaining strong in all weather conditions is one of the main advantages of this knot, making it ideal for use outside.

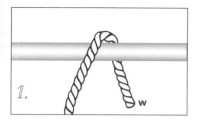

Take the working end of the rope over the post or object.

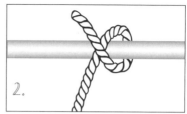

Wrap the end around the post and cross it over the front from right to left.

Take the end of the rope beneath the post again and wrap around, crossing over from left to right and securing the second turn of rope.

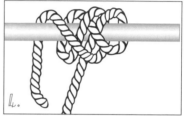

Create another turn around the post ensuring that the loop is inside the right hand turn and crosses in front of the standing part diagonally from right to left.

Complete the last turn diagonally from left to right passing the working end under turn 2.

Tighten so that it forms a square-shaped, flat knot.

Cat's Paw
KNOT

The **Cat's Paw** is a hitch used to connect a rope
to an object securely. It is loosely based on the
Cow Hitch but features additional twists on
each side of the bight, which makes it sturdier
in harsh conditions.
It can be fixed to a pole, rod or hook after it has been tied
and is versatile in the ropes which it works with. For this
reason, it is common in both fishing and pioneering.

1.

Take the middle of a length of rope and create two small loops, leaving a length between the loops.

2.

Take the loop in each hand holding between the thumb and forefinger. Turn away from you to create a twist in each loop.

3.

Continue twisting each loop until the leftmost loop has four clockwise twists, and the rightmost has four anti-clockwise twists.

4.

Pass the two loops over the end of the pole or hook.

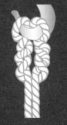

5.

To fasten, pull on both standing ends.

1

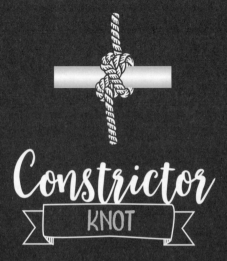

Constrictor
KNOT

The **Constrictor Knot** is an incredibly strong knot that has many useful applications, and is reminiscent of the snake from which it takes its name. It can withstand significant tension and is robust in extreme wet or windy weather. For these reasons, when accompanied with square lashing, it is the ideal knot to use when making a rope ladder. The Constrictor Knot is also advantageous for whipping the end of a rope line if no tape is available and will prevent the ends from fraying. The knot holds well and grips itself so that it is often impossible to untie without cutting the line.

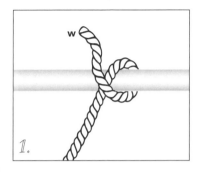

1.

Wrap the end over the object and make a complete turn around the object and then over the front of the standing part.

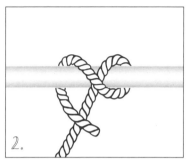

2.

Take the working end around the object to the left of the first loop and back over the standing part.

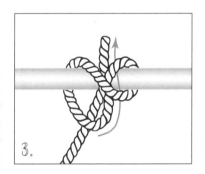

3.

Tucking the working end up through the centre of the X formed by the two loops.

4.

Pull tight to secure.

2

Fisherman's
BEND

Otherwise known as the Anchor Bend, the **Fisherman's Bend** is an especially strong and simple knot that will not buckle under strain and can be untied easily. It is commonly used to fasten a rope to an anchor and it is recommended for this purpose that the free end is seized to prevent the knot from fraying as this will jeopardize its security. Although commonly believed to be a bend, the Fisherman's Bend is actually a hitch. The name is derived from a period when a 'bend' referred to any knot, rather than specifically joining two lines together as we know today.

1.

Pass the end through the eyelet of the anchor or point of attachment.

2.

Make two complete turns of the working end before taking the working end across the standing part and back through the two loops.

3.

Pass the working end over the top of the standing part, and then behind it and thread through to make a half hitch.

4.

Pull down on the knot to fasten.

Prusik
LOOP

An essential part of the Prusik Knot is the **Prusik Loop**, best tied with climbing cord. Although you can buy this loop at most adventure shops, making your own can be cheaper and just as effective. The finished knot should be able to slide along the length of the rope and is the perfect basis for starting the French Prusik Knot.

This example creates a simple Prusik Loop, but it can be further strengthened by using a Double Fisherman's Bend. Always ensure that you consult with an expert before using the Prusik Loop or French Prusik Knot in any climbing activities.

1.

Lay the rope out in a circle and form a loop in one end, this will become your working end.

2.

Thread the loose end through the loop created.

3.

Take the working end and cross it over its own rope and the rope of the standing part.

4.

Wrap the working end around once more, as in Step 3.

5.

Thread the working end through the two loops created.

6.

Pull on the ends to tighten.

1

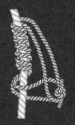

French Prusik
KNOT

A **French Prusik Knot** is a short piece of cord that adds friction, typically used by climbers. They are advantageous in that they can easily slide up and down a rope, but they hold fast when a tension is exerted onto the line. Otherwise known as an Autoblock, the French Prusik is easy to tie and can be released even under a load, making it preferential to use in abseiling. Greater difference in diameter between the two ropes will result in improved performance of this knot.

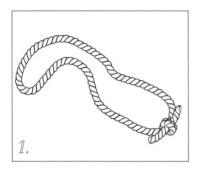

Form a loop in a piece of cord by knotting the loose ends together. A Prusik Loop is recommended for this knot.

Wrap the loop around the object, creating a full turn.

Pass the rope around the object again. Repeat this turning until you have four complete turns.

Pull to tighten and neaten the knot. You can then join the loops together with a carabiner.

2

Taut Line
HITCH

The **Taut Line Hitch** is an adjustable hitch for use on lines subject to pressure. It is unique in that it can be slipped when required, but it firmly holds fast under load. This knot is particularly useful to campers for tying guy lines because the hitch slides freely yet jams under tension.

The Ashley Book of Knots proposes an alternative way of finishing the knot, by reversing the direction of the half hitch in Step 4, which is believed to make the knot less prone to twisting.

1.

Make a turn around the post or object, taking the working end behind the standing part.

2.

Take the working end back over the standing part to create a loop around the standing part. Then repeat to create a second loop.

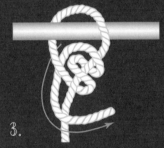

3.

Pass the working end down through and behind the large loop, and across the front of the standing part.

4.

Make one additional turn of the standing part and take the working end up through the loop.

5.

Pull tight, adjust to create a taut line.

Timber
HITCH

As the name suggests, the **Timber Hitch** is used for pulling timber. The knot effectively attaches a single length of rope to a cylindrical object and can support great weight.

The addition of a half hitch forms the slightly more supportive knot, the Killick Hitch, which allows the object to be dragged on land or through water. This extra hitch keeps the timber or object in line as it is towed along. Both hitches are easy to untie once they are no longer required.

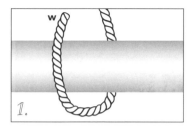

Make a loose turn around the object from the back to the front.

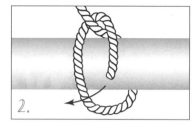

Take the working end and cross it behind the standing end before taking it in front.

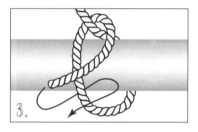

Guide the working end through the loop before bringing it back to the front.

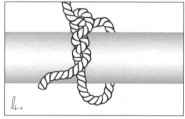

Repeat Step 3 to wind the working end around the turn further.

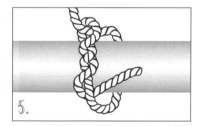

Thread the tip of the working end back through the main turn. Pull to tighten forming the Timber Hitch.

To create a Killick Hitch, draw the standing end away from the existing knot. Create a turn of the timber and form a half hitch before pulling taut to secure both knots.

Blood KNOT

The **Blood Knot** is very efficient at retaining its strength when tied to another line. This knot is fiddly to tie, and therefore if you are new to knots it may be better to practice dexterity with some of the easier knots before jumping in with the Blood Knot.

Acclaimed as the 'best bend for small, stiff or slippery lines' by *The Ashley Book of Knots*, this knot is increasingly popular in fly-fishing. The dexterity required to tie this knot lends it to being best suited to lines with a small diameter, as they tend to be more flexible for creating bends and turns.

1.

Lay two lines flat beside one another.

2.

Take the first line and wrap around the second line four times.

3.

Place the working end between the two lines after wrapping.

4.

Repeat this with the second line wrapping around the first, and thread the working end between the two lines.

5.

Pull tight.

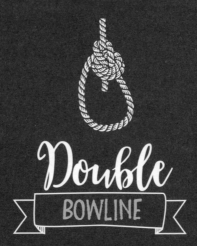

Double
BOWLINE

Drawing on the standard Bowline knot, the **Double Bowline** features the components of the traditional knot but with reinforcements making it well suited for heavy-duty rigging. It is a common misconception that this knot results in a Bowline with two loops, but that is a knot in its own right, known as the Spanish Bowline.
The additional turns in the Double Bowline make this knot significantly less likely to capsize than the basic Bowline.

Create a loop in the line and form a second, smaller loop with the working end.

Make one further turn creating a larger loop and then pass the working end through the two smaller loops from back to front.

Pull through the working end and lay it alongside the standing part.

Pass the working end behind the standing part and thread it back towards the knot passing between the two loops from front to back.

Pull the slack to tighten the knot.

1

The **Carrick Bend** is a knot used to join two lines together. The biggest advantage of the Carrick Bend is that it works well with thick, stiff ropes, making it the preferential type of bend for larger ropes.

It can withstand water and poor weather and will not jam. The two ropes do not have to be of the same diameter.

Dating back to at least 1783, the Carrick Bend is perhaps the closest we can get to the perfect bend. It is symmetrical and easy to tie, and its pleasant appearance complements its practicality.

1.

Form an overhand loop in one of the ropes. It does not matter whether this is the thicker or thinner rope, as the knot is symmetrical if successfully tied.

2.

Lay the second rope over the loop and then beneath the standing part of the first rope, before bringing it over the working end of the first rope.

3.

Take the working end up through the first loop, over its own standing part and back down through the loop.

4.

Both ropes should now be symmetrical. Tighten by pulling the standing parts. If tied successfully, the two loops should sit neatly into each other.

Fisherman's
KNOT

The **Fisherman's Knot** is not a knot, as the name suggests, but a symmetrical bend consisting of two Overhand knots. It has a variety of names including the English Knot, Halibut Knot and Waterman's Knot.

Although most commonly associated with fishing, this knot is prone to slipping in nylon lines, in which case it is recommended to add more turns and form the Double Fisherman's Knot, or even the Triple Fisherman's Knot.

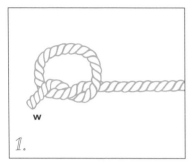
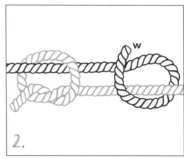

1.

Tie a loose Overhand knot in the end of one rope. Keep the knot small but do not tighten.

2.

Using a second piece of rope, thread the working end through the Overhand knot, before taking it around the standing part of the first rope.

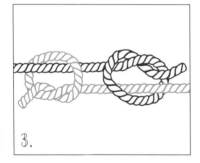
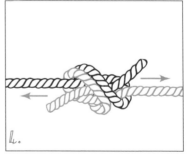

3.

Make an Overhand knot in the second rope. Each standing part should pass through the Overhand knot of the alternate rope.

4.

Pull on the working ends to tighten each knot. Then pull the standing ends in opposite directions so that the knots lie snug against one another.

2

Double Fisherman's
KNOT

The **Double Fisherman's Knot**, otherwise known as the Grapevine Knot, is a bend used to join two lengths of rope. It is an adaptation of the Fisherman's Knot that is able to bear a stronger load and is less susceptible to becoming loose.

This knot is a well-known and reliable knot most commonly used in climbing, and search and rescue. It is also used as a hobby-knot in knitting, net-making and for macramé jewellery.

1.

Lay two ends of rope parallel to one another.

2.

Take the working end of one rope and wrap it twice around the standing part of the other rope. Then thread the working end through the two turns that have just been formed.

3.

Repeat Step 2 with the other rope in the opposite direction by taking the working end twice around the standing part of the alternate rope, and then threading its own working end through the two turns.

4.

The knot should look symmetrical. Pull the two standing ends in opposite directions to tighten the knot.

The Double Fisherman's Knot can be easily adapted to form the Triple Fisherman's Knot by wrapping the rope in Steps 2 and 3 thrice around the object, rather than twice.

5.

Rigger's KNOT

The **Rigger's Knot** is often referred to as the Hunter's Bend, named after its founder Dr Edward Hunter. The knot was only published in the 1970s, making it a relatively contemporary knot. It holds historical importance as it was the knot that prompted the creation of the International Guild of Knot Tyers.

Like all other bends, its primary purpose is to tie two lines together, which it does through interlocking Overhand Knots.

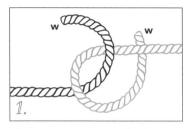

1.

Make two interlocking bights in the working ends of two lengths of rope. Thread one working end beneath its own standing part.

2.

Continue taking this end around beneath the loop of the other line.

3.

Form an Overhand knot by passing this end over itself and down through the loop.

4.

Take the working end of the other line and pass it under itself forming a loop.

5.

Take the working end of the second line through the loop of the first knot, and then through its own loop.

6.

Adjust the knots until the lengths of the working ends are comparable to one another. Pull to tighten.

2

Running BOWLINE

The **Running Bowline** is an effective way of
tying a noose as it can be slid undone easily and will not
bind. As well as being the preferred knot for building a
garden swing, it is also used widely in boating and climbing
for retrieving objects which may have fallen.
This knot can be made with or without access to
the ends of a rope, but if possible, it is easier to
first tie the Bowline and then thread the
standing end through it.

1.

Pass the rope over the pole or object of attachment.

2.

Form a loop in the tail of the working end, and take the working end across the front of the standing line.

3.

Pass the working end around the back of the standing part and then up through the back of the loop.

4.

Thread the working end back around itself, before passing through the larger loop, and back through the smaller loop.

5.

Pull on the standing end to run the bowline tight up to the pole or object.

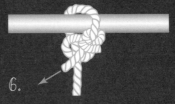

6.

Tighten so that it forms a square-shaped, flat knot.

Surgeon's
KNOT

Unsurprisingly, the **Surgeon's Knot** was originally devised as a surgical knot that worked to bind tissue together during surgery. It is believed to have been used from as early as the first century as evident from Heraklas' monograph on surgical knots and slings. Today, the Surgeon's Knot is used in situations where tension must be maintained on a point of pressure. The knot is susceptible to capsizing if the standing end and working end are pulled apart. Like the Reef Knot, tying this knot can be remembered by:
"Left over right and under, repeat,"
"Right over left and under".

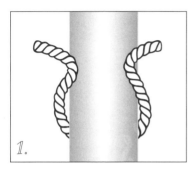

Wrap the rope around the object.

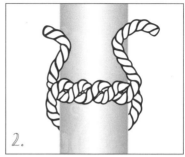

Take the working end from the left over the right and under. Repeat.

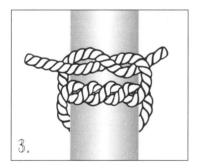

Take the working end from the right over the left and under.

Pull tight.

The **Tape Knot** is also referred to as the Water Knot and is most commonly used in climbing for joining two ends of webbing together. This knot works best to bind leather or tape but could also work with natural or synthetic rope. Although beneficial for climbers when tied correctly, this knot is particularly susceptible to becoming loose if not tied securely or loaded improperly. To overcome this, adding an additional Overhand Knot in the outer strap or using a Flat Overhand Bend are good alternatives to maximize stability.

1.

Form a loop with one strap.

2.

Wrap the working end through its own loop, forming an Overhand Knot.

3.

Thread the other strap in the reverse direction through the loop from front to back.

4.

Loop the working end behind the first knot, over the first strap and beneath its own standing part.

5.

Take the working end over and down through both loops.

6.

Pull both straps to tighten.

2

Zeppelin
BEND

For a general-purpose bend, look no further than the **Zeppelin Bend**. It can be tied using a range of rope and will respond well to both natural and synthetic lines, making it favourable to the Alpine Butterfly. If tied correctly, the ropes will not separate from one another, nor will the knot jam.
The Zeppelin Bend is thought to have secured airships, which were commonly called Zeppelins in dedication to Count Ferdinand von Zeppelin. Understandably, mooring airships exerted a great strain upon the knot, showcasing its reliability and strength.

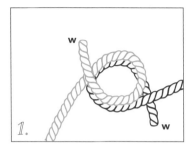

Take two ropes laid on top of each other and bend their working ends over to the right.

Take the working end of the top rope and cross it under its own standing part and up through both loops.

Take the working end of the bottom rope and cross it over its own standing part and down through both loops.

The two working ends of each rope should be in opposite directions, if correct, pull to tighten.

Chain SENNIT

The **Chain Sennit,** otherwise known as Chain Sinnit, is one way of shortening a rope whilst in use. The chain of repeated crochet-like stitches prevents tangling or excess rope becoming caught.

Its most common usage appears in the circus big top as the slack can be quickly released if necessary, making it advantageous for temporary knotting. The chain forms the basis of more elaborate decorative knots, such as the Daisy Chain and Monkey Braid.

1.

Form a loop towards the end of the rope.

2.

Make a bight just beneath the loop.

3.

Feed the bight through the loop hole from back to front. This will form a hanging loop.

4.

Make a second bight and pass it from back to front through the hanging loop.

5.

Continue creating bights and threading them from back to front through the previous hanging loop until you have tied the excess rope.

6.

When the last hanging loop has been tied, thread the working end through it. Pulling on the working end will collapse the rest of the rope and release the knot.

Chinese Button

KNOT

Button knots have been in use for centuries and the **Chinese Button Knot** has been used primarily on clothes in Asia. Their flat composition makes them more comfortable against the body than common composition buttons, and for this reason they are often used on underwear or nightwear as a stopper knot or for decorative purposes.

The traditional design has five loops which are tightened to form a spherical shape. However, tightening four of the five loops leaves one surplus for hanging, for example on earrings or pendants.

Make a large bight in the middle of a rope.

Take the curved section of the bight and fold it in half on itself towards the standing part to form a double loop.

Slightly overlap the two loops.

Hold the intersection of the two loops between the thumb at the front and the forefinger at the back.

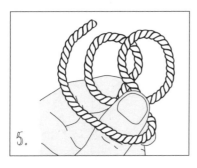

Take the working end over your thumb and behind up through the left loop.

Weave the working end from front to back, threading it through the intersection made in Step 3 and then up through the right loop.

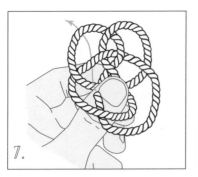

Take the working end up through the back of the loop where the thumb is and down through the loop directly above.

Tighten the knot by working the knot, carefully pulling the slack while maintaining the shape.

When the knot is almost tight you can create a square shape by pushing up the sides of the knot.

Alternatively you can tighten further by pushing the edges down to create a more rounded shape. You may need to tease out the centre strand of the knot if this hidden.

2

Jury Mast
KNOT

Just as the name suggests, the **Jury Mast Knot** is traditionally used to jury rig a temporary mast onto a ship or boat in the event of the original one failing. The knot is designed to hold the makeshift mast upright, but it can also be used in camping to secure tents or flagpoles.

To secure the Jury Mast onto a rigging, place the centre of the knot over a pole or spar and tie both standing ends. The three bights are used as attachment points to hold the knot fast. The Jury Mast is not only practical but also decorative and can be stitched onto clothing for aesthetic appeal. These instructions show one of the three possible variations.

1.

Form three crossing turns, ensuring that the working end is crossing beneath the standing end each time. The loops should be of comparable size and overlap their left neighbour.

2.

Take your left hand beneath the left edge of the leftmost loop, over the second turn and grab the third. In short: the left hand goes under, over and grabs. Repeat this with your right hand on the right side, but pass over the outer loop, beneath the second loop and grab the third. In short: the right hand goes over, under and grabs.

3.

Pull on the two pieces of rope you are holding from Step 2. They should form separate loops either side of the main knot.

4.

Pull the bights to neaten the Jury Mast knot.

Plait
SENNIT

The **Plait Sennit** is known by many other names including the Plait Sinnit, Braid Sennit, Pleat, and Plat. They also vary in complexity from the simple three-ply braid, often used for plaiting hair, through to more decorative variations such as the nine-strand Sennit Braid.

Sennit is widely used in Oceania for its applications in traditional architecture, straw weaving, boat building, fishing, and as ornamentation.

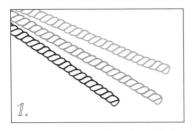

1.

Lay three pieces of cord parallel to one another. Differing thicknesses and lengths can be used but the finished knot will look neater if similar cord is used.

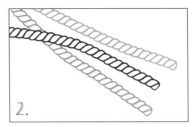

2.

Pass the left rope over the middle rope.

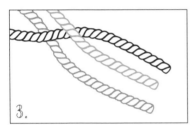

3.

Pass the right rope over the middle rope.

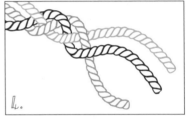

4.

Continue the sequence by repeating Steps 2 and 3 and tighten the braid from time to time.

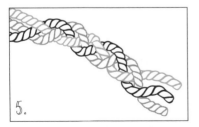

5.

Once the desired length has been reached, finish the knot off with a Constrictor Knot, or a Stopper Knot.

2

Square
KNOT

The **Square Knot** is a decorative Japanese knot often used in Macrame. It forms the foundation of most basic Macrame knots and is sometimes referred to as the Japanese Crown or Japanese Success Knot.

This knot is relatively simple to tie because of its symmetrical nature and has been used traditionally to represent balance and friendship. Nowadays, the knot is widely used in Scout and Guide circles for tying neckerchiefs in place of the traditional woggle.

1.

Form a bight towards the end of one rope and pass the working end of the other rope through it from back to front.

2.

Thread the working end back beneath the bight.

3.

Pass the working end from beneath the bight to encircle the bight by passing it above itself.

4.

Use the working end of the first rope and thread it over the existing bight and through the bight made in Step 3.

5.

The square knot is now formed. Carefully pull on all lines simultaneously to work the knot tight and maintain its shape. If desired, the ends can be trimmed to result in an even knot.

True Lovers'
KNOT

Just like the Square Knot, the design of the **True Lovers' Knot** is symbolic of friendship and balance, and this tradition dates back to the 5th century AD. For this reason, the knot often appeared on jewellery and rings to depict flexibility around a loved one, but also represents strong unity.

Common legend has it that a young couple's love would last as long as the knot would hold. Today, the knot is primarily used for decorative purposes as it is prone to jamming when under pressure and risks becoming undone without exerted tension.

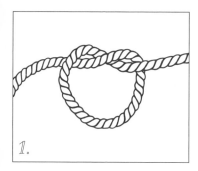

Create an overhand knot in one line but do not pull tight.

Thread the working end of a second line through the centre of the overhand loop and pull through, creating a second loop that interlocks the first.

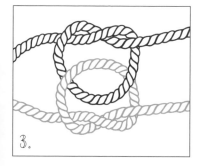

Tie an overhand knot in the second line at the point it interlocks with the first. You should have two interlocking overhand knots.

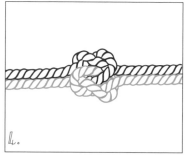

Finish the knot by pulling the ends in opposite directions.

3

Turk's Head
KNOT

The **Turk's Head Knot** is a decorative knot comprising of interwoven strands that form a closed loop. Most often this knot is tied around an object, such as a pole or spar, making it a popular knot in sailing. For decorative purposes, however, it is often recommended to be tied flat (to weave an attractive rug) or tied spherical (as in a Monkey's Fist). Today, the most common uses for the Turk's Head are in Scouting and Guiding associations or as a fire-starting tool. Although it can prove beneficial in reducing friction, the knot does not have many practical uses.

1.

Take the working end of a rope over and around an object such as a pole or spar. Cross the rope over itself and take it behind the object.

2.

Thread the working end beneath the object and under its own standing part.

3.

Twist the pole towards you a ¼ turn. Then take the working end over and under towards the right. You now have three lines.

4.

Take the left line and pull it over the middle line. Then take the working end over the middle line and under the left line.

5.

Twist the pole towards you and next to the standing end take the working end over the middle cord and under the right line.

6.

Pull through to complete the knot. You can double up by taking the working end through the same path.

2

Bottle
SLING

The **Bottle Sling** provides a handle for carrying bottles, jars or jugs and is often used in survival situations. However, the sling can be tied to a boat to cool drinks in cold water, but this relies upon a greater length of cord.
Only one length of cord is required for this knot, and it is recommended that parachute cord be used as it can be untied easily to remove the bottle.

Make a large bight in the middle of a rope.

Take the curved section of the bight and fold it in half on itself towards the standing part to form a double loop.

Slightly overlap the two loops.

Take the central point of the bight and pass it under the left hand standing end, down through the intersection and over the right loop to form a new bight.

Take the top loop at the front of the bight and pull this down. Next take the loop that is behind the bight and pull down behind the knot.

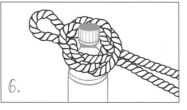

Pull to tighten around the neck of the bottle.

1

Cow
HITCH

The **Cow Hitch** or Lanyard Hitch is similar to the Clove Hitch, but the second half is reversed – neither knot should be trusted alone for critical applications. The Cow Hitch is less likely to bind than the Clove Hitch, but just as likely to jam.

The common alternative name for this knot, the Lark's Head, comes from Bowling's *The Book of Knots* in 1866 and is a literal translation from a French manuscript.

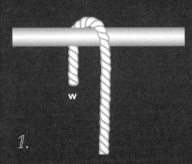

1.

Pass the rope around an object and back around itself.

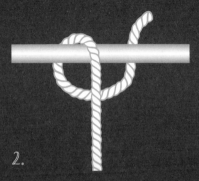

2.

Take the working end behind the standing end of rope.

3.

Thread the working end over the object on the opposite side and down through the loop, resting against the standing end.

③

Eye
SPLICE

Creating an **Eye Splice** involves the unravelling and reweaving of rope to create a permanent fixed Flemish Eye at the end of a three-strand rope. Although not technically a knot, the Eye Splice is useful to know for instances that require a rope to be slipped over a hook or object. Instructions for Eye Splicing can vary depending on the type of rope used, and it is recommended that three tucks are necessary for natural fibres whereas synthetic line requires at least five tucks. To maximize the durability of an Eye Splice, incorporate a thimble into the finished eye.

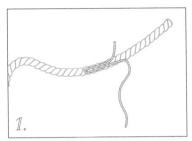

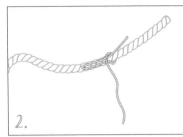

To prevent the entire line unravelling, it is recommended to first whip the rope by taking whipping twine and forming a bight on the end of a rope.

Wrap the working end of the whipping twine around its own bight and the larger rope, working away from the rope's end.

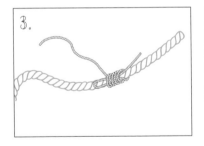

Continue winding the whipping twine until it spans an inch (2.5cm) in diameter.

Thread the end of the whipping twine through its own loop, and trim both ends. You have now whipped the rope.

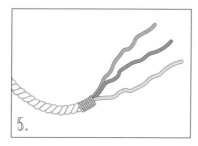

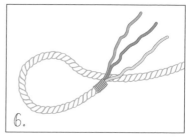

Unwind the rope into separate strands up to the whipping, this example demonstrates how to whip a three-strand rope.

Create a loop in the end of the rope. This will form the eye of the finished splice.

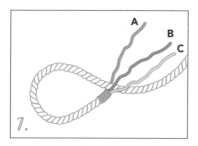

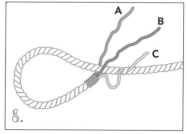

Take Strand A beneath the standing part, and Strand B over the standing part.

Take Strand C and thread it through one of the strands on the main rope – this will hold the loop in position. Pull Strand C through and tight.

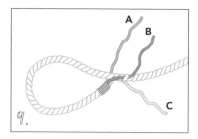

Pull Strand C to the right and repeat Step 8 using Strand B to thread above the previous one. Pull through and tighten.

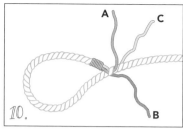

Flip the splice 180° horizontally and move Strand B to the right. Repeat Step 8 using Strand C to thread above the previous one. Pull through and tighten.

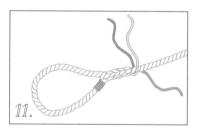

Using steps 8–10, alternate between going over one strand and underneath the next. Pull tight and flip 180° after each set of tucks.

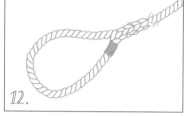

To finish the splice, cut the ends close and heat-seal on synthetic ropes, or cut the ends long on natural ropes.

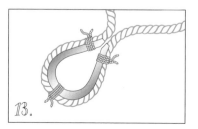

To improve durability, fitting the eye with a thimble reduces the wear on the rope.

Sheepshank
KNOT

The **Sheepshank Knot** serves to shorten a rope without the need for cutting it, making it extremely useful in bypassing a weakened section of line. The section you want to isolate should sit in the centre of the 'S'.

Boy Scouts have been required to learn this knot for hundreds of years, but it isn't very applicable to everyday use due to uncertainties about its stability. Instead, the Alpine Butterfly is the preferred knot to use in critical environments such as climbing, search and rescue or sailing.

1.

Make a bight in the rope and then an inverted bight to form an 'S' shape.

2.

Take the top working end over the lower bight to wrap over, and then underneath itself before passing through the loop.

3.

Take the lower working end over the upper bight to wrap over, and then underneath itself before passing back through the loop.

4.

Pull to tighten.

5.

If the ends are free to go through the loops, the knot will be more secure if each working end is passed through the loop end.

Tom Fool's
KNOT

The **Tom Fool's Knot** is so-named because those caught in its handcuff-like loops were deemed a 'Tom Fool'. This knot was thought to be inescapable and makes it a common choice for tethering animals.

The speed with which this knot can be tied is its main advantage, and for this reason it is commonly used to serve as a pair of handcuffs over the similar Handcuff Knot. If tied correctly, the loops are easily adjustable by pulling on the standing ends.

In the middle of the line, make a loop that lies clockwise and crosses behind the standing part.

To the right of the loop, make another loop anticlockwise taking the working end behind.

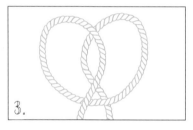

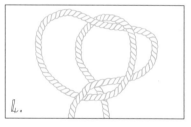

Overlap the two loops so that the rightmost loop is beneath the left.

Take the right side of the left loop and pull it through the right loop from front to back.

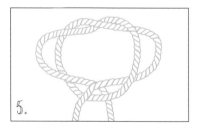

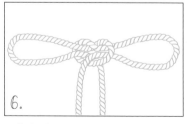

Take the left side of the right loop and pull it through the left loop from back to front.

Pull the loops in opposite directions to tighten.

INDEX

BIBLIOGRAPHY

Falconer's Universal Dictionary of the Marine by William Falconer, published by London (1769)
Knotting Matters by the International Guild of Knot Tyers (1987)
The Ashley Book of Knots by Clifford W Ashley, published by Faber & Faber (1993)
The Book of Knots by Tom Bowling, published by Robert Hardwicke (1866)
Reeds Knot Handbook: A pocket guide to knots, hitches and bends by Jim Whippy, published by Bloomsbury (2011)
Knot Know-How: How to Tie the Right knot for every job: A New Approach to Mastering Knots and Splices by Steve Judkins, published by Fernhurst Books (2003)
Knots (Collins Gem) by Trevor Bounford, published by Collins (2005)
Bear Grylls Survival Skills Handbook: Knots by Bear Grylls, published by Bear Grylls (2017)
Knots and Splices by Steve Judkins, published by Fernhurst Books (2013)

OTHER GREAT TITLES FROM RYDON PUBLISHING

The No.1 Book of Numbers
Ruth Binney
ISBN: 978-1 910821-17-6

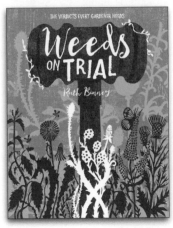

Weeds on Trial
Ruth Binney
ISBN: 978-1 910821-27-5

www.rydonpublishing.co.uk
www.rydonpublishing.com